# Letterboxes

## of

## Australia

Thank you to the home owners who proudly display their letterboxes to the public and who have made this book possible.

Australia's postal service was officially born on 25 April 1809, when a former convict named Isaac Nichols was appointed to take charge of all mail arriving in what was then called the Colony of New South Wales. Isaac Nichols opened Australia's first post office at his home in George Street in Sydney, NSW. He began advertising in the "Sydney Gazette" (the equivalent of a newspaper in those days) the names of all those who were fortunate enough to receive mail. The people listed could collect their letters from Nichols' home by paying the fixed price of a shilling per letter, with parcels costing more depending on how heavy they were. High-ranking (very important) members of the community received personal deliveries from Nichols.

Early letters were written on a piece of paper which was then folded and secured with a wax seal. Some people had "signet rings" that they used to press their very own "coat of arms", or other special design, into the seal. Envelopes are a more recent invention.

Australia's earliest overland mail routes were operating by the late 1820s, with regular packhorse and coach deliveries travelling from Sydney to nearby townships such as Parramatta, Penrith, Liverpool and Windsor in New South Wales.

The first Australian postcards went on sale at the Sydney GPO in New South Wales in 1875

In 1883 Melbourne and Sydney were finally linked by rail and people began receiving their letters within a day or two of posting them.

In 1911, the Postmaster General launched a national design competition for the nation's first stamp. The Postmaster General at the time, Charles Frazer, personally hoped for a stamp projecting a bold, modern image, and preferably featuring an outline map of Australia. His wish was that every letter leaving Australia's shores should have an "advertisement of the country on its stamp".

After months of planning and revision, it was decided that the first Commonwealth stamps would feature a simple design depicting an image of a kangaroo inside a map of Australia. The kangaroo image chosen had actually won equal second prize in the competition and was designed by Edwin Arnold from England.

Christmas stamps were released for the first time in 1957, making Australia the first country in the world to issue Christmas stamps every year since.

In 1967, four-number postcodes were given to every suburb in Australia to assist with the sorting of letters by machines.

In 1980, Posties stopped blowing whistles to announce to people that they had put mail in their letterboxes.

In 1991 Australia Post introduced an Express Post service. This guaranteed delivery of an item for the next business day if mailed from one capital city to another.

In 1999, Australia Post introduced its barcode sorters – machines that can "read" barcoded addresses on small letters and then automatically sort them. This was followed by the installation of large-letter sorting machines in the five mainland capital cities.

More letters were sent in Australia in 2007/08 than at any other time in our nation's history.

Australia Post's retail network is the country's largest, with around one million customers served every business day.

For more history and information on the Australian Postal system go to
http://auspost.com.au/education/ourpost/students/our-post/timeline.html

Let's take a look at a tiny number of the different letterboxes which can be found throughout this country........

*Miss*

*Suburbia*

**The stylish letterbox which doubles as a direction beacon to your front door when she lights up at night**

# Mr & Mrs Caravan Park

**There is no mistaking the mail meant for these**

# Mr History

**A blast from the past matches the Victorian home**

# The Jurassic

**Watch the fingers!**

# The Social Club

**Commonly found at the end of country lanes**

# The Bird House

**A resting place for Carrier Pigeons?**

Peek -a -Boo

Room for letters but nothing else

# The Rusty Milk Can

### Works for farmers

# By the Seaside

**One way of keeping the house safe**

*Miss*

*Fashionable*

**Always color co-ordinated with the home**

# Master

# Machinery

**Mail has arrived, the wheels of communication are in motion.**

# Yeehaw!

**This is *Cowboy* country**

# The Eagle has Landed

*Wagon Ho!*

*A Postman Friendly Pooch?*

# From the 70s

When letterboxes were a part of the garden.

# The Entertainers

*Mr.*

*Kelly*

**At Your Service**

Down On
the Farm

# For the Kids

He's
watching
you

# Saddle Up

**One for letters,
one for parcels**

*Christmas*

*Cheer*

# Divine

# Communication?

**Have you ever noticed, Churches don't have letterboxes?**

www.ingramcontent.com/pod-product-compliance
Lightning Source LLC
Chambersburg PA
CBHW060809290526
45792CB00005BA/1582